SABBATH MOOD HOMESCHOOL
PRESENTS

Living Science Study Guides
A Charlotte Mason Resource for Exploring
Science, a Vast and Joyous Realm

FORM 2 WEATHER
(GRADES 4-6)

Accompanying the book
Junior Science Book of Rain, Hail, Sleet & Snow by Nancy Larrick

"But for the most part science as she is taught leaves us cold; the utility of scientific discoveries does not appeal to the best that is in us, though it makes a pretty urgent and general appeal to our lower avidities. But the fault is not in science——that mode of revelation which is granted to our generation, may we reverently say?——but in our presentation of it by means of facts and figures and demonstrations that mean no more to the general audience than the point demonstrated, never showing the wonder and magnificent reach of the law unfolded."

-CHARLOTTE MASON, *TOWARDS A PHILOSOPHY OF EDUCATION*.

Introduction

In this Form 2 Weather study guide, students will learn about cloud formation and type, various types of precipitation and humidity, wind, lightning and thunder, hurricanes and tornadoes, the cause of seasonal differences in weather, and the difference between weather and climate.

Spine Text
This study guide accompanies the living book *Rain, Hail, Sleet & Snow* by Nancy Larrick (Living Library Press, 2016.)

- 63 pages
- Reading Level: 4-7 grade

Author Bio
Nancy Larrick (1910-2004) was many things and did many things. A teacher in her hometown of Winchester, Virginia where she grew up and a teacher in many different countries of the world. A lover of nature, collector of rare children's books, passionate about history, and a fan of felines. She is credited with bringing to the attention of our nation the absence of ethnically diverse characters in the books young people read. This was in 1965 during the Civil Rights movement, setting into motion much needed change that is still going on today.

She wrote five books herself and edited many more. She always sought the advice and recommendations of young people when she was collecting poetry for one of her 20+ anthologies of poetry for children. Allowing them to help choose titles and allowing them to be free to write their own poems.

She loved the written word and the sounds, rhythm, and feelings of those words. She wanted all to know the beauty of the written and spoken word. Most of all she loved people. Especially those who "are doing things and asking questions". (Jahncke, Michele)

Necessary Titles to Complement This Course
- *Handbook of Nature Study* by Anna Botsford Comstock
- A "nature lore" book. See a list of options on page 5.
- A "special study" book. See a list of options on page 6.

Exams
You can download a digital copy of the exam questions for this study at https://qrs.ly/z5cpfou.

Broken Links
If you notice a broken link in this study guide, please email the author for a replacement: Nicole@SabbathMoodHomeschool.com.

Schedule
This study guide includes 33 lessons, three per week, each requiring 20-30 minutes. Each week will include the following lessons:
- Lesson 1: Nature Lore
- Lesson 2: Natural History Science Reading and sometimes an activity
- Lesson 3: Special Studies Reading or Natural History Activity

Other necessary science and nature study should be done during afternoons or evenings, and may include the following:

- Daily work outside exploring and investigating, making notes or drawings of observations. Due to the subject matter of this study guide, some of this daily work will need to be done after sunset.
- Additional reading on this science topic and nature topics according to individual desire and interest.

Science Notebook

A science notebook is unnecessary at this level, but an oral, written, or drawn narration is required after every reading or activity.

Science is one of the most challenging subjects to narrate because it is not as narrative as other subjects. Your student's science narrations may seem disjointed, or it may seem as though they have missed a significant amount of the material. Remember that while the facts and details in a living science book are clothed in living language, there are still many facts and details.

Nature Notebook

Students must keep a nature notebook with daily notes or drawings of their special study topics and any other things they observe in nature. Their notes can include specific observations or questions about their investigations. They may also like to include items such as poems, calculations, or records of consecutive measurements.

This notebook should reflect their style and personality and should never be judged or graded. Teachers should make encouraging remarks about their student's observations, questions, and efforts, not about the quality of their drawings.

Suggested Activities to Complement This Course

If possible, organize a field trip to your local television station to talk to the meteorologist.

Nature Lore Suggestions

"The real use of naturalists' books at this stage is to give the child delightful glimpses into the world of wonders he lives in, to reveal the sorts of things to be seen by curious eyes, and fill him with desire to make discoveries for himself."

-CHARLOTTE MASON, *HOME EDUCATION*, P.64

The Story Book of Science by Jean Henri Fabre (Yesterday's Classics, 2006, 432 pp.) is comparable to the nature lore book Charlotte Mason assigned in this category. Students should read approximately eight chapters per term over three years.

There are several alternatives listed below, in case your student has already read *The Storybook of Science.* Just be sure you only schedule 35-40 pages per term.

- *Life and Her Children* by Arabella Buckley (328 pp. Charlotte Mason used this in Form 2.)
- *Madam How and Lady Why* by Charles Kingsley (180 pp. Charlotte Mason used this in Form 2 sometimes.)
- *The Secret of Everyday Things* by Jean Henri Fabre (381 pp. A good alternative.)
- *The Lay of the Land* by Dallas Lore Sharp (214 pp. also good.)
- *Nearer Nature: The Secrets of a Wildlife Watcher* by Jim Arnosky (160 pp. A good option, but shorter.)
- *The Lay of the Land* by Dallas Lore Sharp (214 pp.)
- *Animal Life in Fields and Garden* by Jean Henri Fabre (412 pp.) (Very good but more difficult.)
- *Insect Adventures* by Jean Henri Fabre (298 pp.)
- *The Burgess Book of Nature Lore* by Thornton Burgess (246 pp.)
- *Small Worlds: Communities of Living Things* by Howard Smith (180 pp.)
- *Squirrels and Other Fur-Bearers* by John Burroughs (132 pp.)
- *Among the People Series* by Clara Dillingham Pierson (pond, farmyard, night, forest, meadow)
- *Animals on the Move* by Ann Sutton (128 pp.)
- *Strange Companions in Nature* by Olive Earle (64 pp.)
- *How Animals Live Together* by Millicent Selsam (95 pp.)
- *All About Animals and Their Young* by Robert McClung (148 pp.)
- *Discovering Plants* by Glenn Blough (48 pp.)
- *The Good and the Beautiful Nature Reader–Insects & Arachnids* by various authors (173 pp.)

Special Studies

"They keep records and drawings in a Nature Note Book and make special studies of their own for the particular season with drawings and notes."

-CHARLOTTE MASON, *PHILOSOPHY OF EDUCATION*, p. 219

Charlotte Mason directed students to make special studies each month, with drawings and notes made daily. Although students pick a topic to study, families, or groups including children of various ages, may wish to focus on a common subject. For example, if the general subject is birds, a young child may just look for all the birds he can, while an older child may choose to study a specific bird, the flight patterns of birds, or their nests and nesting habits.

Visit SabbathMoodHomeschool.com for a prepared Special Studies Rotation. (https://qrs.ly/uecize3)

Special Study Book Suggestions

"Our main dependence is on books as an adjunct to out-of-door work...In these books the children are put in the position of the original observer of biological and other phenomena. They learn what to observe, and make discoveries for themselves, original so far as they are concerned. They are put in the right attitude of mind for scientific observations and deductions, and their keen interests awakened."

-CHARLOTTE MASON, *SCHOOL EDUCATION*, p. 238

Once a special study topic is chosen, gather some books that your students can read independently on that subject. Some weeks there is time allotted in the morning schedule to read their chosen book, but students may also read them during their leisure time. Any of the following authors would be excellent, but as their books are often out of print, they can be expensive. See if your library can find you a copy through interlibrary loan.

- Robert McClung
- William Long
- Clara Dillingham Pierson
- Glenn Blough
- Jean Craighead George

- Alice Goudey
- Jim Arnosky
- Olive Earle
- Herbert Zim
- Margaret Waring Buck

Leisure Reading Suggestions

Your students may like to read more about this science topic during their free time, so choose a few of the following books to purchase or check out from your local library.

- *Close to the Wind: The Beaufort Scale* by Peter Malone (32 pp.)
- *Snowflake Bentley* by Jacqueline Briggs Martin (32 pp.)
- *Snowflakes in Photographs* by W. A. Bentley (Bentley's photographs)
- *My Brother Loved Snowflakes: The Story of Wilson A. Bentley, the Snowflake Man* by Mary Bahr (32 pp.)
- *Snow* by Thelma Harrington Bell
- *Not Only for Ducks: The Story of Rain* by Glenn Orlando Blough (46 pp.)
- *On the Same Day in March: A Tour of the World's Weather* by Marilyn Singer (40 pp.)
- *Sunshine Makes the Seasons* by Franklyn M. Branley (LRFO 2)
- *Follow the Water from Brook to Ocean* by Arthur Dorros (LRFO 2)
- *The Story of the Trade Winds* by Ruth Brindze (68 p.)
- *Storms* by Melvin Berger - 1977 version (48 p.)
- *Climate Maps* by Ian F. Mahaney (24 p.)
- *Miss Pickerell and the Weather Satellite* by Ellen MacGregor (157 p.)
- *Danny Dunn and the Weather Machine* by Jay Williams (144 p.)
- Find more living books on the weather page at SabbathMoodHomeschool.com.

Supply List

If you are gathering supplies for the whole course, the following list should be helpful. If you will instead gather supplies for each lesson, see the Teacher Prep page for each week.

Find a digital list and links to suggested products at
www.SabbathMoodHomeschool.com/form-2-supply-lists.

HomeScienceTools.com or supply store
Compass
Eye Dropper or pipette
Magnifying glass (optional)
Pliers or tongs
Windsock

Hardware Store or Hobby Store
Outdoor thermometer

Grocery Store
Balloon (option 1, see week 5)
Brown paper lunch bag (or a balloon and stick pin)
Drinking straw
Superglue

Around the house
Aluminum foil, three 12 x 12 inch (30 x 30 cm) squares (option 2, see week 5)
Black paper
Cloud chart: Cloud Identification Guide by Dr. Tina Cartwright of Marshall University and/or Cloud Identification Chart from the National Aeronautics and Space Administration and/or Cloud Identification Chart from Globe.gov. You may wish to print these double-sided and then laminate them, so they stay in good condition throughout the term.
Heat source, such as a light bulb or electric burner
Ice cubes
Light source (lamp, flashlight)
Marker
Metal pie or cake pan
Notebook paper or a sheet of plastic, such as a transparency sheet (option 2, see week 5)
Paper plate or construction paper
Pine cone
Quart size, wide-mouth Mason jar, with lid (1 liter)
Scissors
Spoon (option 1, see week 5)
Stick pin
Water
Wax paper or parchment paper
Wool cloth (option 2, see week 5, mittens, socks, or a sweater will work)

TEACHER PREP

01 Prepare to do an object lesson on the weather.

- Review the appendix to this guide to familiarize yourself with the list of object lessons available.
- Based on the weather forecast this week, choose an object lesson that you will do with your child.
- Write a few of the questions listed in the lesson on a piece of paper for reference when you go outside for a nature walk.

02 Gather the supplies needed for this week's activities. (See the supply list on page 8 for a link to suggested supplies.)

- Outdoor thermometer
- Print one or more of the following cloud charts. You may wish to laminate them, so they stay in good condition throughout the term.
  - Cloud Identification Guide (https://qrs.ly/tpcmxxg) by Dr. Tina Cartwright of Marshall University.
  - Cloud Identification Chart (https://qrs.ly/mgcmxy1) from the National Aeronautics and Space Administration.
  - Cloud Identification Chart (https://qrs.ly/qicmxyk) from Globe.gov.
- Windsock

03 Schedule your weekly nature walk and outside time.

- In addition to *daily* time outside, students should take a nature walk at least *once a week*.
- Consider including some friends for accountability, or your family may like to go alone. (Or a variety of both from week to week.)
- Choose one or more places to walk. A rotation of 3-4 locations adds interest.
- Be prepared. It will make a difference if everyone is appropriately dressed, has their own water bottle, and if you have a backpack with items that may be needed, such as band aids and snacks.
- Don't take your nature notebooks into the field. Instead, ask your kids to narrate about your walk on the way home and then make a nature notebook entry upon their return.

- Please don't turn it into a time of teaching. You may do an object lesson while you are out there, but for the most part, let the children make discoveries for themselves and do not feel compelled to answer all of their questions.
- Does the idea of getting your kids outside *daily* to play and explore and going for a nature walk *weekly* feel overwhelming? For some encouragement, read the article "The Value of Nature Study" on SabbathMoodHomeschool.com. (https://qrs.ly/rdcjwf0)

Lesson 1: Nature Lore

Time: 20 minutes

Read: Nature Lore book; 3-4 pages

Narration: Ask your student for a narration from this reading. You may request that he say it aloud, write it down, or draw a narration.

Afternoon Occupation

Choose Special Study #1: Go outside with your child, either in your backyard, your neighborhood, or someplace you would be willing to travel to several times a week. Look around you, and think about what special study you would like to make this term. Talk to your child about what he sees that he would like to know more about. Remember that the object should be observed daily; therefore, if it is a time of year when the weather is harsh, choose something that your child can observe during a quick walk outside, is visible through a window, or can be kept indoors.

For more guidance and a prepared rotation, see the notes in the introduction of this book.

Charlotte Mason's students commonly made two or three special studies per term. The weather will be one of those this term and what you select this week will be another. You will also be prompted to choose a second topic later in the term.

Lesson 2: Natural History

Time: 20 minutes

Show your student the painting on the next page. Allow 2-3 minutes for him to look closely at all the details in the picture. Then ask him to tell you about it.

Did your student notice the clouds? Why are some areas of the ground well lit and others shaded? Why did the artist include such a large proportion of sky compared to land? Does it look like there will be a storm?

Student Read (or teacher if necessary): *Rain, Hail, Sleet & Snow*, chapter 1 "Clouds Tell the Story."

Narration: Ask your student for a narration from this reading. You may request that he say it aloud, write it down, or draw a narration.

For Discussion: Is your student eager to learn about the weather? Is there something he hopes to learn? Ask what makes him curious.

Afternoon Occupation

Special Study: Have your child take a few minutes to study the object he has chosen and then make notes and possibly a drawing in his nature notebook of something he has observed.

View of Haarlem with Bleaching Grounds by Jacob Isaakszoon van Ruisdael (1665)
Source: [Public domain], via Wikimedia Commons

Lesson 3: Activity

Time: 30 minutes

Weather is the combination of sunlight, wind, snow or rain, and temperature in a particular region at a particular time. By having a few weather instruments available, you can record the weather in your neighborhood each day.

Activity: Prepare a simple weather station.

Supplies Needed—

- Outdoor thermometer
- Cloud chart
- Windsock
- Compass
- Pine cone
- Superglue
- Drinking straw

Procedure—

1. Prepare a chart to record your weather throughout this term.
   a. A piece of binder paper will work well, as it already has horizontal lines.
   b. Separate the page into eight columns and label each column as follows: Date, Temperature, Cloud Cover, Type of Clouds, Precipitation, Wind Direction, Wind Speed, Humidity.
2. Date: Record today's date on the first line of your chart.
3. Temperature: Hang the outdoor thermometer in a permanently shaded location and then record the temperature on your chart.
4. Cloud Cover: Is it clear, cloudy, partly cloudy, or overcast? Note it on your chart.
5. Type of Clouds: Determine what kinds of clouds you see by looking at your cloud identification guide.
6. Precipitation: Is it raining or snowing? Do you see dew, frost, or fog? Note it on your chart.
7. Wind Direction: Wind direction is noted according to where the wind is coming from. For instance, a wind that blows from the north is known as a "north wind." Use a compass to determine which direction your windsock is blowing. Using that information, determine which direction the wind is coming from. Note it on your chart. (e.g., NW or SW)
8. Wind Speed: Attach your windsock to a tree or a flag pole. Note the number of Reflective Fluorescence Belts that are erect due to the wind

pushing through the windsock. If you would like to calculate the actual speed of the wind according to your windsock, follow the instructions in the article "How to Determine Wind Speed Using a Windsock" over several days. (https://qrs.ly/flcmxyp)

9. Pine cone Humidity Reading: Super Glue the tip of a drinking straw to the top of an open pine cone scale. Place the pine cone on a window sill, and note the position of the straw. It is pointing up = high humidity; pointing to the side = low humidity.

Hang your chart in a convenient place and record the weather on it daily.

Narration: Ask your student to explain what he did during this activity and why. You may request that he say it aloud, write it down, or draw a narration.

Afternoon Occupation

Nature Study: Finalize your plan for a special study. If you have already settled on an object, take time to look at it together, and instruct your child to make notes and/or drawings in his nature notebook.

TEACHER PREP

01
Prepare to do an object lesson on the weather.

- Review the appendix to this study guide to familiarize yourself with the topic of the weather, and the list of object lessons available.
- Based on the weather you are likely to experience this week, choose an object lesson to complete with your child.
- Write 3-4 of the questions listed in the lesson on a piece of paper for reference when you go outside.

02
Gather the supplies needed for this week's activities.

- Quart size, wide mouth Mason jar, with lid (1 liter)
- 1/4 cup (60 ml) warm water
- 6-8 ice cubes

03
Order books from the library.

- You might already own books on the subject your child has chosen for his special study. If not, then check out a few from the library. Please do not limit your selections because once you get home, you might find that a book you picked is not as appealing as it first seemed. Also, look for a few titles from the list of leisure reading options in the introduction.

04
Schedule your weekly nature walk and outside time.

- Read the article, "Nature Walks, Excursions, and Rambles – part 1" on SabbathMoodHomeschool.com to learn how to encourage "*satisfactory intellectual results*" when you lead your kids on a nature walk. (https://qrs.ly/5mcjwf2)

Lesson 1: Nature Lore

Time: 20 minutes

Read: Nature Lore book; 3-4 pages

Narration: Ask your student for a narration from this reading. You may request that he say it aloud, write it down, or draw a narration.

Afternoon Occupation

Special Study #2 (the weather): Take a nature walk with your child this afternoon. Ask him to notice the weather. Then, using the list you prepared, ask your child a few questions. Your goal is to secure his attention and draw from him a new understanding of the subject. Instruct your child to make notes and/or drawings in his nature notebook of the things he observes. If your child needs help, offer to record his narration of what he saw into his nature notebook for him.

"*The purpose of so-called object-lessons is to assist a child, by careful examination of a given object, to find out all he can about it through the use of his several senses. General information about the object is thrown in, and lodges only because the child's senses have been exercised and his interest aroused.*" —Charlotte Mason, Parents and Children, p. 180

Lesson 2: Natural History

Time: 20 minutes

Ask your student what he remembers from the last time he read *Rain, Hail, Sleet & Snow*.

Have you ever noticed that each time you look at the sky, the clouds appear different? Even as you lay on a blanket and watch them steadily, they change before your eyes. Sometimes you can see shapes in them. Possibly a rabbit or an elephant. Have you also noticed that sometimes they are very tall, while other times they are only wisps across the sky as if someone has pulled a cotton ball apart? They can be bright white against a brilliant blue sky or dark gray and angry looking. The clouds can tell you what the weather will be like. Suppose you were planning a picnic this afternoon. What kinds of clouds would predict rain or snow? What kind of clouds would ensure a nice day?

Student Read (or teacher if necessary): *Rain, Hail, Sleet & Snow*, chapter 2 "All Kinds of Clouds."

Narration: Ask your student for a narration from this reading. You may request that he say it aloud, write it down, or draw a narration.

For Discussion: Ask your student what kind of clouds he sees in the sky today. Can he tell what kind of weather they might bring?

Optional Activity: Watch the StudyJams video, "Weather & Climate." (https://qrs.ly/79cmxzj, 4:17 min.)

Afternoon Occupation

Special Study: Have your child take a few minutes to study the object he has chosen and then make notes and possibly a drawing in his nature notebook of something he has observed.

Lesson 3: Activity

Time: 30 minutes

Activity: Create a cloud.

Supplies Needed—

- Quart size, wide mouth Mason jar, with lid (1 liter)
- 1/4 cup (60 ml) warm water
- 6-8 ice cubes

Procedure—

1. Pour warm water into a jar.
2. Set the lid upside down over the opening of the jar.
3. Place ice in the tray created by the lid.
4. Watch what happens inside the jar.
5. After a minute or two, you can lift the lid to look at the bottom side of it. You may see condensation that will create rain.
6. Replace the lid and allow a few minutes to pass.
7. Watch for tiny drops of water to form on the inner sides of the jar indicating a cloud has formed. Notice where the drops form? (The top, middle, or bottom of the jar.)
8. Watch for rain to drip down.

The clouds in the sky form in the same way. Warm air from close to the earth rises up into the sky, where it cools, and condenses into rain clouds.

Narration: Explain what steps you took to create a cloud.

Afternoon Occupation

Nature Study: Have your child take a few minutes to observe his special study object or nature in general. Then make notes and possibly a drawing in his nature notebook of what he has observed. If you haven't completed an object lesson yet this week, do so today.

TEACHER PREP

01 Prepare to do an object lesson on the next plant or animal of your child's chosen special study.

- Look in the Table of Contents (page xv,) of the *Handbook of Nature Study* (*HoNS*) for the topic. (I bookmarked the contents page so I can return to it easily.)
- You will find a list of animals in part II and a list of plants in part III.
- Read the informational section specific to the subject to be studied, as well as any applicable lessons on the topic.
- Write a few of the questions listed in the lesson on a piece of paper for reference when you go outside for a nature walk.
- If possible, you will do an object lesson about this topic several weeks in a row, so you will not need to cover all of the questions in one lesson.

02 Gather the supplies needed for this week's activities.

- None needed

03 Schedule your weekly nature walk and outside time.

- Remember that nature study is the foundation for science. "*If the great world of nature, its phenomena, forces, and laws, is ever to be made a subject of study, there is no time better than childhood for beginning that study; because there is no time when the pupil is more easily interested in natural objects. Wait until the child has reached adult age, and is capable of mastering all the 'ologies' and 'onomies,' and probably there will be no taste for such subjects to animate the study.*" (Moore, Rev. H. H. "Forgotten Pioneer of a Rational Education and His Experiment", *The Parents Review*, vol. 15, 1904, p. 263)
- Where will you go for a nature walk this week? What day? Will your family go alone or will you invite a friend?

Lesson 1: Nature Lore

Time: 20 minutes

Read: Nature Lore book; 3-4 pages

Narration: Ask your student for a narration from this reading. You may request that he say it aloud, write it down, or draw a narration.

Afternoon Occupation

Special Study: Have your child take a few minutes to study the object he chose to make a study of in week one. Conduct an object lesson by asking him some of the questions you read in *HoNS* about the topic. Ask him to make notes and possibly a drawing in his nature notebook of something he has observed.

Lesson 2: Natural History

Time: 20 minutes

Ask your student what he remembers from the last time he read *Rain, Hail, Sleet & Snow*.

Whoever wrote the rhyme, "Rain, rain go away, come again another day," didn't know how fun the rain can be to play in. Have you ever stood outside as the rain began to fall and felt it splatter on your face or the palms of your hands? Have you built a boat out of a piece of bark and floated it in a mud puddle? Have you inspected a spider web that is glistening with raindrops? Today you will learn how rain is formed in the sky, and why sometimes it falls from the clouds we see and sometimes it doesn't.

Student Read (or teacher if necessary): *Rain, Hail, Sleet & Snow*, chapter 3 "Rain, Rain, Rain."

Narration: Ask your student for a narration from this reading. You may request that he say it aloud, write it down, or draw a narration.

For Discussion: If it is cold outside, ask your student to blow his warm breath against a cold window as suggested in the text on page 23. If it is not cold outside, ask how he could cause a piece of glass to be cold enough to test this idea.

Afternoon Occupation

Special Study: Have your child take a few minutes to study the object he has chosen and then make notes and possibly a drawing in his nature notebook of something he has observed.

Lesson 3: Special Study Reading

Time: 30 minutes

Read: Special Study book; student read for about 10 minutes.

Narration: Ask your student for a narration from this reading. You may request it be oral, written, or drawn.

Afternoon Occupation

Nature Study: Have your child take a few minutes to observe his special study object or nature in general. Then make notes and possibly a drawing in his nature notebook of what he has observed. If you haven't completed an object lesson yet this week, do so today.

Painting the Skies: If your child has an interest, read John Muir Laws' article, "How to Paint Skies with Watercolor I." (https://qrs.ly/qtcmxzv) Particularly notice his technique for using a white or clear crayon or birthday candle to block clouds.

TEACHER PREP

01
Prepare to do an object lesson on the next plant or animal of your child's chosen special study.

- Write a few of the questions listed in the lesson on a piece of paper for reference when you go outside for a nature walk.

02
Gather the supplies needed for this week's activities.

- None needed

03
Schedule your weekly nature walk and outside time.

- Periodically suggest that the kids bring home an object to paint in their nature notebooks. Instruct them to choose something *common* rather than a rare object. Some fun collections include leaves, acorns, pine cones, pressed flowers, sea shells. Remember, don't take anything from places that don't allow collecting.
- Be cautious that your own negative feelings about nature study do not hinder your child's interest. Charlotte Mason said, "*Some children are born naturalists, with a bent inherited, perhaps, from an unknown ancestor; but every child has a natural interest in the living things about him which it is the business of his parents to encourage; for, but few children are equal to holding their own in the face of public opinion; and if they see that the things which interest them are indifferent or disgusting to you, their pleasure in them vanishes, and that chapter in the book of Nature is closed to them.*" — *Home Education*, p. 58

Lesson 1: Nature Lore

Time: 20 minutes

Read: Nature Lore book; 3-4 pages

Narration: Ask your student for a narration from this reading. You may request that he say it aloud, write it down, or draw a narration.

Afternoon Occupation

Special Study: Have your child take a few minutes to study his chosen object. Conduct an object lesson by asking him some of the questions you read in *HoNS* about the topic. Then make notes and possibly a drawing in his nature notebook of something he has observed.

Lesson 2: Natural History

Time: 20 minutes

Ask your student what he remembers from the last time he read *Rain, Hail, Sleet & Snow.*

Blow, blow, thou winter wind,
Thou art not so unkind
As man's ingratitude;
Thy tooth is not so keen,
Because thou art not seen,
Although thy breath be rude.
Heigh-ho! sing, heigh-ho! unto the green holly:
Most friendship is feigning, most loving mere folly:
Then, heigh-ho, the holly!
This life is most jolly.

Freeze, freeze, thou bitter sky,
That dost not bite so nigh
As benefits forgot:
Though thou the waters warp,
Thy sting is not so sharp
As friend remembered not.
Heigh-ho! sing, heigh-ho! unto the green holly...

— William Shakespeare

Student Read (or teacher if necessary): "Where Does the Wind Come From?" on the following page.

Narration: Ask your student for a narration from this reading. You may request that he say it aloud, write it down, or draw a narration.

Activities:
- Study the Beaufort scale on page 29 with your student and use it to determine how hard the wind is blowing today.
- View a wind map (https://qrs.ly/yzcmxzy) of the wind being experienced across the United States currently, or look at a worldwide wind map. (https://qrs.ly/a2cmy0h) To change the view, click on the word "earth" in the bottom left of the screen and change "projection" to "W3."

Afternoon Occupation

Special Study: Have your child take a few minutes to study the object he has chosen and then make notes and possibly a drawing in his nature notebook of something he has observed.

Where Does the Wind Come From?

Have you ever felt the wind on your face on a warm summer day? It cools your skin and makes you feel comfortable. But in the winter, when the air is bitter cold, the wind can make you feel even colder. You may wish for the wind to quit blowing at a time like that, but that is not a good idea. What if the air on earth did become still right this moment? If it is raining at your house, the storm would just remain there. But what about the farmer in the next state? If the rain clouds stay over your house and never move over to his crops, there will be no food to eat in the coming months. Think also of the seeds and animals that use the wind to travel.

The wind is an important element of the weather. Weather forecasters track the direction the wind is blowing and the speed it is blowing. If you hang up a windsock or put a weather vane on the top of your roof, you will know from which direction the wind is coming. If it is coming from the north, it is called a north wind, and if it is coming from the south, it is called a south wind. It is easy to remember the name of the wind. If a person is from Canada, they are said to be Canadian. That is where they are from. The wind is also named by where it comes from.

By determining the direction of the wind, weather forecasters know something about what kind of weather is coming your way. If you live in the northern hemisphere, a north wind is sure to bring cooler weather from further up north. A southern wind will bring warmer weather from the south.

Have you ever wondered what causes the wind to blow? The sun causes it. The sun warms the earth's surface, both the land and the water. The warm air then rises upward. As it goes up, it pushes the cool air above it back down to the surface of the earth, where it then begins to warm up. It is a cycle that works similar to the Ferris wheel at the fair. As warm air rises, cool air moves down, and it is this movement of air that we call the wind.

You may be wondering how the sun can cause the wind even if you cannot see the sun through the clouds, or maybe it is nighttime, and still the wind blows. Some winds are created in a single place, but most wind is formed over large portions of the earth. The speed of the wind is also important. That can be determined by using an *anemometer*, a device used to measure wind speed. Still, it can also be determined by observing how the wind affects your surroundings. Sir Francis Beaufort created a wind speed scale so sailors could better record the wind speeds while sailing. Today that scale has been adapted for use on land.

The sun may warm the land in Brazil, pushing warm air up over Texas, which then cools and moves down over Missouri. That is why you may feel the wind on your face when the sun is nowhere in sight.

Beaufort Scale

Force	Description	Events on Land	MPH
0	Calm	Smoke rises vertically	<1
1	Light air	Direction of wind shown by smoke, but not by wind-vane	1-3
2	Light breeze	Wind felt on face; leaves rustle; wind-vane turns to wind	4-6
3	Gentle breeze	Leaves and small twigs in motion; wind extends small flags	7-11
4	Moderate breeze	Wind raises dust and loose paper; small branches move	12-18
5	Fresh breeze	Small leafy trees start to sway; wavelets with crests on inland waters	19-23
6	Strong breeze	Large branches in motion; whistling in telephone wires; difficult to use umbrellas	24-30
7	Near gale	Whole trees in motion; difficult to walk against wind	31-36
8	Gale	Twigs break from trees; difficult to walk	37-44
9	Strong gale	Slight structural damage to buildings; chimney pots, tiles and aerials removed	45-52
10	Storm	Trees uprooted; considerable damage to buildings	53-61
11	Violent storm	Widespread damage to all types of buildings	62-70
12	Hurricane	Widespread destruction; only specially constructed buildings survive	≥71

Lesson 3: Special Study Reading

Time: 30 minutes

Read: Special Study book; student read for about 10 minutes.

Narration: Ask your student for a narration from this reading. You may request it be oral, written, or drawn.

Afternoon Occupation

Nature Study: Have your child take a few minutes to observe his special study object or nature in general. Then make notes and possibly a drawing in his nature notebook of what he has observed. If you haven't completed an object lesson yet this week, do so today.

Painting the Skies: If your child has an interest, read John Muir Laws' article, "How to Paint Skies with Watercolor II." (https://qrs.ly/f4cmy14)

TEACHER PREP

01

Read a portion of the *Handbook of Nature Study* (*HoNS*).

- Write out a few more questions from the lesson on the special study topic your child is focusing on. Use these questions for reference when you go outside for a nature walk.
- If there are no more questions to write down from this lesson, see if there is another lesson that is related or considers the topic in a more general way. For instance, if your student has been studying Queen Anne's Lace (Lesson 148,) which is one of the specific weeds covered in *HoNS*, then you can look back at Lesson 135: Outline for the Study of a Weed.

02

Gather the supplies needed for this week's activities.

- A brown paper lunch bag (or a balloon and stick pin)

Option #1:
- A balloon
- A spoon

Option #2:
- A piece of notebook paper or a sheet of plastic, such as a transparency sheet
- Three 12 x 12 inch (30 x 30 cm) squares of aluminum foil, folded into a flat disc that is approximately 3 inch (7 cm) square
- A piece of wool cloth (such as wool mittens, socks, or a sweater)
- A helper

03

Schedule your weekly nature walk and outside time.

- Read the article "Nature Walks, Excursions, and Rambles – part 2" on SabbathMoodHomeschool.com to learn what you should do (have a goal, provide direction) and what you shouldn't do (lecture, take nature notebooks along) when you go on a nature walk. (https://qrs.ly/zrcjwfd)

Lesson 1: Nature Lore

Time: 20 minutes

Read: Nature Lore book; 3-4 pages

Narration: Ask your student for a narration from this reading. You may request that he say it aloud, write it down, or draw a narration.

Afternoon Occupation

Special Study: Have your child take a few minutes to study the object he has chosen and then make notes and possibly a drawing in his nature notebook of something he has observed. Conduct an object lesson by asking him some of the questions you read in *HoNS* about the topic.

Lesson 2: Natural History

Time: 20 minutes

Ask your student what he remembers from the last time he read *Rain, Hail, Sleet & Snow.*

A lightning rod on the house intercepts a lightning strike. It safely carries the current of electricity around the outside of the house and into the ground. When lightning strikes a home without a lightning rod, the lightning travels into the house, possibly starting a fire.

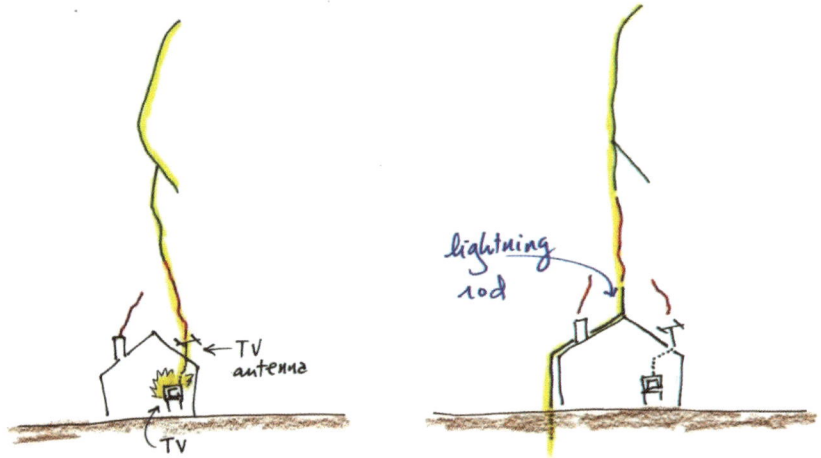

Source: University of Arizona, [CC BY 4.0], via Wikimedia Commons

Student Read (or teacher if necessary): *Rain, Hail, Sleet & Snow,* chapter 4 "A Flash of Lightning and a Clap of Thunder."

Narration: Ask your student for a narration from this reading. You may request that he say it aloud, write it down, or draw a narration.

For Discussion: In the text, the author says, "*To escape electricity in the open, it is best to lay flat in a hollow away from a lone tree.*" The current National Weather Service recommendations disagree with those instructions to some degree. However, they do not have clear suggestions for what you should do if you are caught outside in a thunderstorm. (They agree that you should stay away from a lone tree and get away from high places, but they say never to lie flat on the ground.) What they do suggest is that you immediately move inside a substantial building when you hear thunder. While there, you should stay off a corded phone, stay out of the bathroom, and stay away from windows.

Optional Activity: Watch the StudyJams video, "Air Pressure & Wind." (https://qrs.ly/7ocmy1t, 3:35 min.)

Lesson 3: Activity

Time: 30 minutes

Activity: Make your own lightning and thunder.

Supplies Needed—

PART 1

   Option #1
- A balloon
- A spoon

   Option #2
- A piece of notebook paper or a sheet of plastic, such as a transparency sheet
- Three 12 x 12 inch (30 x 30 cm) squares of aluminum foil, folded into a flat disc that is approximately 3 inch (7 cm) square
- A piece of wool cloth (mittens, socks, or a sweater will work)
- A helper

PART 2
- A brown paper lunch bag (or a balloon and stick pin)

Procedure—This activity will work best on a low humidity day.

PART 1

Option #1:
1. Rub a balloon on your head or on your cat.
2. Move a spoon near the balloon until you see or hear a small spark

Option #2:
1. Position the paper on a flat surface and ask your helper to hold it in place.
2. Rub the paper with the wool, using quick, firm strokes, for at least 45 seconds. (Count to 45 or set a timer.)
3. Place one piece of folded foil on the center of the sheet of paper.
4. Ask your helper to lift the paper off the surface.
5. Touch the metal and watch for a spark.
6. Repeat using a different piece of folded aluminum foil.

You created a tiny spark of static electricity. By rubbing the balloon against your hair, the balloon stole electrons from your hair. That left your hair positively charged and the balloon negatively charged. The turbulent conditions within a cloud cause this to happen as particles of water and ice collide. As the cloud fills up with electrically charged particles, the lighter, positively charged particles rise to the top of the cloud. The heavier, negatively charged particles sink to the bottom of the cloud. Eventually, the positive and negative charges grow large enough to jump through the air in a sudden rush of electrons from one conductor to another. That may happen within the cloud or from the cloud to the positively charged ground. In your experiment, the electrons jumped from the balloon to the spoon.

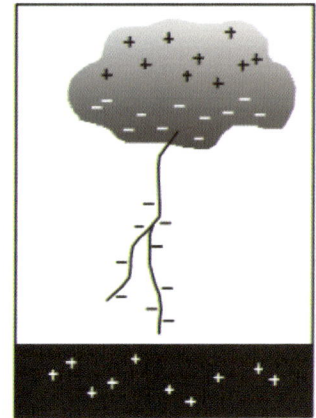

PART 2

When you created a spark, did you hear a slight crackle? Thunder is caused by the air expanding and contracting very rapidly.

1. Blow up a brown paper lunch bag
2. Twist the open end and close with your hand.
3. Quickly hit the bag with your free hand.
4. Alternatively, blow up a balloon, tie a knot to close it off, and then poke it with a pin.

The quick pressure you applied to the bag caused it to break and the air inside the bag to rush out. In doing so, it pushed the air outside away from the bag, where it continued to move forward in a wave until it reached your ear, causing you to hear a sound. Thunder is produced similarly. When lightning jumps, it heats the nearby air and causes it to expand rapidly. This fast air movement causes the crash of thunder that you hear when you see a flash of lightning.

Do you know which travels more quickly, light or sound? The lightning and thunder are happening simultaneously, but light reaches you instantly, while the sound takes longer. You can determine the distance you are from the lightning strike by counting the number of seconds between the flash of lightning and the crack of thunder. (Use a stopwatch or count "One-Mississippi, Two-Mississippi, Three-Mississippi," etc.) Every 5 seconds you count means the storm is one mile away. For example, if you counted to 10, you can divide that number by 5 to discover that the strike was only two miles away.

For Discussion: Ask your student if he has ever been shocked by static electricity? Can he explain why it happened?

Narration: Ask your student to explain what he did during this activity and why. You may request that he say it aloud, write it down, or draw a narration.

This activity was adapted from NOVA Teachers: Lightning! StemWorks: Thunder.

TEACHER PREP

01 Prepare to do an object lesson on the weather.

- Review the appendix to this study guide to familiarize yourself with the topic of the weather, and the list of object lessons available.
- Based on the weather you are likely to experience this week, choose an object lesson to complete with your child.
- Write 3-4 of the questions listed in the lesson on a piece of paper for reference when you go outside.

02 Gather the supplies needed for this week's activities.

- None needed

03 Schedule your weekly nature walk and outside time.

- Remember that nature study is the foundation for science: "*[S]et him face to face with a thing, and he is twenty times as quick as you are in knowledge about it; knowledge of things flies to the mind of a child as steel filings to magnet...Now, consider what a culpable waste of intellectual energy it is to shut up a child, blessed with this inordinate capacity for seeing and knowing, within the four walls of a house, or the dreary streets of a town.*" —Charlotte Mason, *Home Education*, p. 67-68

Lesson 1: Nature Lore

Time: 20 minutes

Read: Nature Lore book; 3-4 pages

Narration: Ask your student for a narration from this reading. You may request that he say it aloud, write it down, or draw a narration.

Afternoon Occupation

Special Study (the weather): Instruct your child to observe his special study object. Then, using the list you prepared, ask him some questions to foster an interest in looking at the thing more closely on his own. If your child needs help, offer to record his narration into his nature notebook for him.

Lesson 2: Natural History

Time: 20 minutes

Ask your student what he remembers from the last time he read *Rain, Hail, Sleet & Snow.*

The life cycle of a hurricane can last several days or even weeks. As meteorologists track them using satellite technology, they need a way to identify each storm system. The World Meteorological Organization has developed a list of hurricane names for the major ocean basins worldwide. Each season the first tropical storm has an A name, the second a B name, and so on throughout the letter W. If there are more than 21 tropical storms in a season, additional storms will be given names from the Greek alphabet. There are six lists of names for the Atlantic Ocean, six lists for the Eastern North Pacific, and four lists for the Central North Pacific. The lists are rotated through, and names are retired only if a storm caused considerable damage or deaths.

Tornadoes, by contrast, are never named. Ordinarily, they last only a few minutes, so forecasters have very little time to warn those in danger. Also, there are over 1000 tornadoes in the U.S. each year, so the list of names would be quite long.

Student Read (or teacher if necessary): *Rain, Hail, Sleet & Snow,* chapter 5 "Tornadoes and Hurricanes."

Narration: Ask your student for a narration from this reading. You may request that he say it aloud, write it down, or draw a narration.

For Discussion: Do you live in an area prone to hurricanes or tornadoes? If so, does your family have a plan for how to stay safe if one occurs in your area?

Activity: Use the chart on the following page to compare and contrast the characteristics of hurricanes and tornadoes. Which do you think is the worst kind of storm?

Although these two weather phenomena are very different, it is incredible to realize that individual storm clouds within hurricanes may generate tornadoes as a hurricane makes landfall. That causes double trouble for people who live in the path of the storm. Still, the combined injuries and deaths per year caused by tornadoes and hurricanes do not equal those caused by thunderstorms in the United States.

Afternoon Occupation

Special Study: Have your child take a few minutes to study the object he has chosen and then make notes and possibly a drawing in his nature notebook of something he has observed.

A Comparison of Hurricanes and Tornadoes

	Hurricanes	Tornadoes
Where they form	Over warm water in tropical zones of the Atlantic and Pacific oceans	Over land and have been spotted on all continents except Antarctica
How big they are	Can be up to several hundred miles wide	Usually no more than 1/2 mile wide
How long they last	Can last up to 3 weeks	Usually last no more than an hour
How strong the winds are	Usually less than 180 mph	Can be up to 300 mph
Forms of Precipitation	Rain	Rain, sleet, and hail
Occurrences per year	10-15 per year	1200 per year in the US alone
Advance warning from forecasters	Several days warning	Usually no more than 15-30 minutes warning
Detection	Pulse-Doppler radar, photogrammetry, and ground swirl patterns	Pulse-Doppler radar, photogrammetry, and ground swirl patterns
Direction of rotation	Clockwise in the southern hemisphere and counterclockwise in the northern hemisphere	Clockwise in the southern hemisphere and counterclockwise in the northern hemisphere
Shape	Symmetrical with clearly defined center	Cone shape

Lesson 3: Special Study Reading

Time: 30 minutes

Read: Special Study book; student read for about 10 minutes.

Narration: Ask your student for a narration from this reading. You may request it be oral, written, or drawn.

Afternoon Occupation

Nature Study: Have your child take a few minutes to observe his special study object or nature in general. Then make notes and possibly a drawing in his nature notebook of what he has observed. If you haven't completed an object lesson yet this week, do so today.

Painting the Skies: If your child has an interest, read John Muir Laws' article, "How to Draw Cloud Shapes." (https://qrs.ly/12cmy24) Particularly notice his technique for using a white or clear crayon or a birthday candle to block clouds.

TEACHER PREP

01 Prepare to do an object lesson on the weather.

- Review the appendix to this study guide to familiarize yourself with the topic of the weather, and the list of object lessons available.
- Based on the weather you are likely to experience this week, choose an object lesson to complete with your child.
- Write 3-4 of the questions listed in the lesson on a piece of paper for reference when you go outside.

02 Gather the supplies needed for this week's activities.

- Wax paper or parchment paper
- Metal pie or cake pan
- Water
- Eyedropper

- Black paper
- Light source (lamp, flashlight)
- Magnifying glass

03 Schedule your weekly nature walk and outside time.

- Your children should be making nearly daily entries in their nature notebook. Read the article, "Nature Notebooks: A Pageant of the Seasons" to learn the *what, when, why, and how* of nature notebooking. (https://qrs.ly/zicjwfj)

Lesson 1: Nature Lore

Time: 20 minutes

Read: Nature Lore book; 3-4 pages

Narration: Ask your student for a narration from this reading. You may request that he say it aloud, write it down, or draw a narration.

Afternoon Occupation

Special Study (possible new topic): Charlotte Mason's students commonly made two or three studies per term. Consider whether your child is ready for a new topic or if it is enough to continue with the studies he is already making. Just be sure that daily observation and weekly object lessons are not becoming a drag because the subject has lost its appeal.

If you decide to include a third topic, then take a nature walk with your child, look around, and think about what would be a good study for this time of year. Talk to your child about what he sees that he would like to know more about.

Lesson 2: Natural History

Time: 20 minutes

Ask your student what he remembers from the last time he read *Rain, Hail, Sleet & Snow*.

Many people don't recognize the difference between hail and sleet. If a hard pellet of ice falls from the sky, they think it is hail. In today's reading, you will learn how to tell the difference.

Hail   Sleet   Glaze

Student Read (or teacher if necessary): *Rain, Hail, Sleet & Snow*, chapter 6 "Hail, Sleet and Glaze."

Narration: Ask your student for a narration from this reading. You may request that he say it aloud, write it down, or draw a narration.

Activity: Study the diagram on the next page. Based on what you learned in today's lesson, can you explain what this image is depicting?

Prepare for the next lesson: Please look ahead to the next lesson, so you will be prepared to start earlier in the day if needed.

Afternoon Occupation

Special Study: Have your child take a few minutes to study the object he has chosen and then make notes and possibly a drawing in his nature notebook of something he has observed.

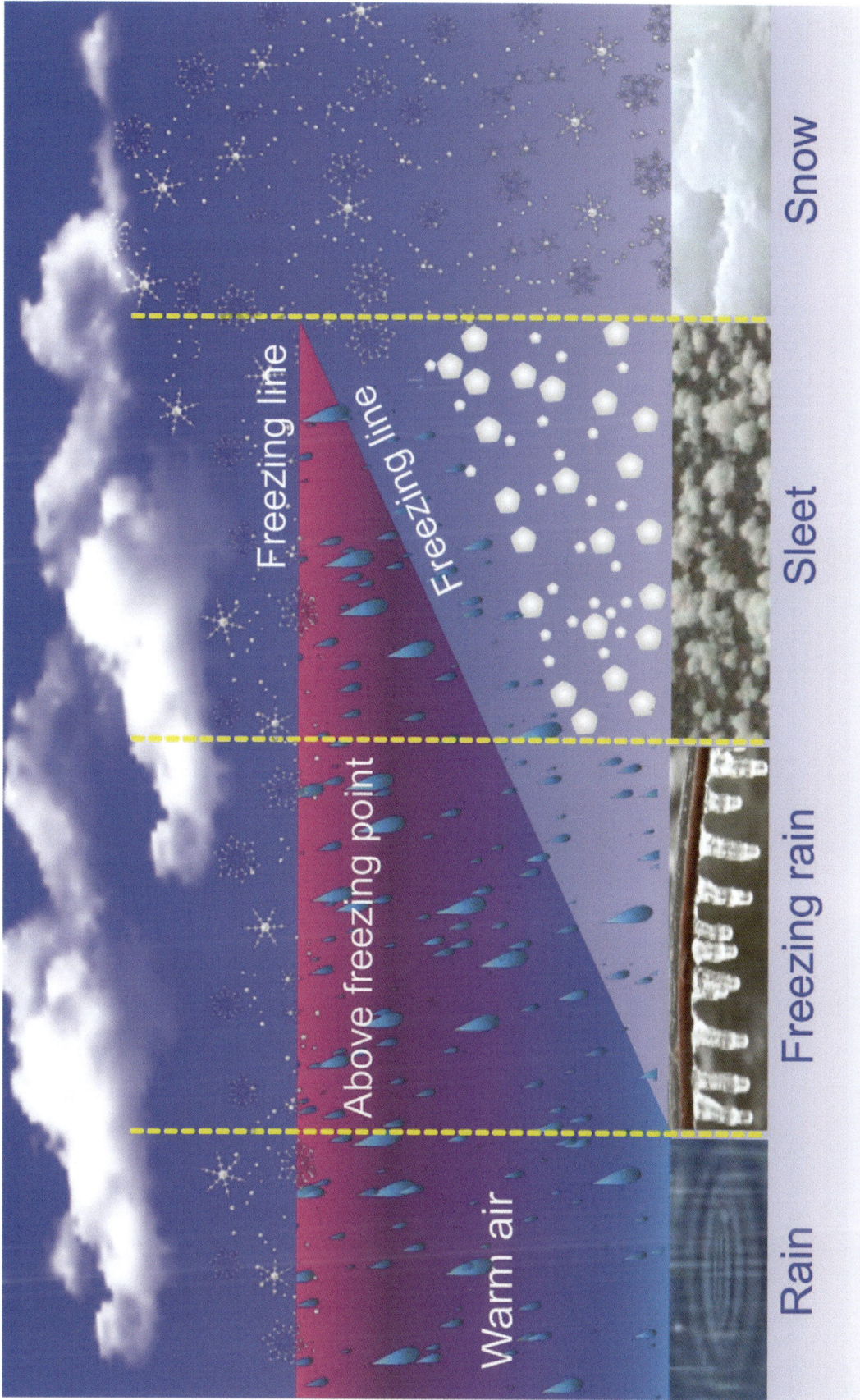

Freezing line

Freezing line

Above freezing point

Warm air

Snow

Sleet

Freezing rain

Rain

Lesson 3: Activity

Time: 4 hours total; 10 minutes every 30-60 minutes.

Please Note—This activity takes several hours to prepare, so you may wish to start it first thing in the morning. You can complete steps 4-7 between morning lessons.

Activity: Make hail.

Supplies Needed—

- Wax paper or parchment paper
- Metal pie or cake pan
- Cold water, even ice water
- Eyedropper
- Black paper
- Light source (lamp, flashlight)
- Magnifying glass

Procedure—

1. Place a piece of wax paper or parchment paper in the bottom of the pie pan.
2. Using an eyedropper, squeeze five small drops of water on the wax paper, about 2 inches from each other.
3. Place the pie pan in the freezer.
4. After 30 minutes, remove the pan and place another drop of water on each of the five initial drops. (If the water is not very cold, it will melt your original frozen drops.)
5. Place the pan back in the freezer.
6. Repeat steps 4 and 5 several more times.
7. Wait one hour after you added the last drop
8. Remove one of the pellets from the pan and place it on a piece of black paper under a light source with the flat side facing up.
9. Leave your other pellets in the freezer so they will still be frozen when the one you are working with melts.
10. Use a magnifying glass to observe the structure of the ice.
11. Replace your pellet with a frozen pellet if it begins to melt.

Narration: Describe what you have observed.

This activity was adapted from *Janice VanCleave's Weather.* Layered.

36

TEACHER PREP

01 Prepare to do an object lesson on the weather.

- Review the appendix to this study guide to familiarize yourself with the topic of the weather, and the list of object lessons available.
- Based on the weather you are likely to experience this week, choose an object lesson to complete with your child.
- Write 3-4 of the questions listed in the lesson on a piece of paper for reference when you go outside.

02 Gather the supplies needed for this week's activities.

- *Snowflake Bentley* by Jacqueline Briggs Martin and *Snowflakes in Photographs* by W. A. Bentley. (optional)

03 Order books from the library.

- You might already own books on the subject your child has chosen for his special study. If not, then check out a few from the library. Please do not limit your selections because once you get home, you might find that a book you picked is not as appealing as it first seemed. Also, look for a few titles from the list of leisure reading options in the introduction.

04 Schedule your weekly nature walk and outside time.

- *"As soon as he is able to keep it himself, a nature-diary is a source of delight to a child. Every day's walk gives him something to enter: three squirrels in a larch tree, a jay flying across such a field, a caterpillar climbing up a nettle, a snail eating a cabbage leaf, a spider dropping suddenly to the ground, where he found ground ivy, how it was growing and what plants were growing with it, how bindweed or ivy manages to climb."* —Charlotte Mason, *Home Education*, p. 54

Lesson 1: Nature Lore

Time: 20 minutes

Read: Nature Lore book; 3-4 pages

Narration: Ask your student for a narration from this reading. You may request that he say it aloud, write it down, or draw a narration.

Afternoon Occupation

Special Study (the weather): Instruct your child to observe his special study object. Then, using the list you prepared, ask him some questions to foster an interest in looking at the thing more closely on his own. If your child needs help, offer to record his narration into his nature notebook for him.

Lesson 2: Natural History

Time: 20 minutes

Ask your student what he remembers from the last time he read *Rain, Hail, Sleet & Snow.*

"How full of the creative genius is the air in which these are generated!

I should hardly admire more if real stars fell and lodged on my coat."

—Henry David Thoreau, *Journal*, 1856

Student Read (or teacher if necessary): *Rain, Hail, Sleet & Snow*, chapter 7 "Snow."

Narration: Ask your student for a narration from this reading. You may request that he say it aloud, write it down, or draw a narration.

Activity: Read *Snowflake Bentley* by Jacqueline Briggs Martin and *Snowflakes in Photographs* by W. A. Bentley OR look at the photographed images of snowflakes on SnowCrystals.com. (https://qrs.ly/p6cmy2f) What do you think of when you see these beautiful crystals?

Afternoon Occupation

Special Study: Have your child take a few minutes to study the object he has chosen and then make notes and possibly a drawing in his nature notebook of something he has observed.

Lesson 3: Special Study Reading

Time: 30 minutes

Read: Special Study book; student read for about 10 minutes.

Narration: Ask your student for a narration from this reading. You may request it be oral, written, or drawn.

Afternoon Occupation

Nature Study: Have your child take a few minutes to observe his special study object or nature in general. Then make notes and possibly a drawing in his nature notebook of what he has observed. If you haven't completed an object lesson yet this week, do so today.

Painting the Skies: If your child has an interest, read John Muir Laws' article, "How to Draw Clouds in Perspective." (https://qrs.ly/i4cmy94)

TEACHER PREP

01
Prepare to do an object lesson on the next plant or animal of your child's chosen special study.

- Look in the Table of Contents (page xv,) of the *Handbook of Nature Study* (*HoNS*) for the topic. (I bookmarked the contents page so I can return to it easily.)
- You will find a list of animals in part II and a list of plants in part III.
- Read the informational section specific to the subject to be studied, as well as any applicable lessons on the topic.
- Write a few of the questions listed in the lesson on a piece of paper for reference when you go outside for a nature walk.
- If possible, you will do an object lesson about this topic several weeks in a row, so you will not need to cover all of the questions in one lesson.

02
Gather the supplies needed for this week's activities.

- None needed

03
Schedule your weekly nature walk and outside time.

- In the article "Nature Walks, Excursions, and Rambles – part 2" assigned as Teacher Prep in week 5, you learned about aims or goals for your nature walks. (https://qrs.ly/zrcjwfd) Make a goal for your walk this week. (e.g. count flowers, find insects, find the biggest and smallest leaves, find objects from each color of the rainbow, look for mushrooms, moss or fungi, watch birds, look for animal tracks, hunt for rocks, etc.)

Lesson 1: Nature Lore

Time: 20 minutes

Read: Nature Lore book; 3-4 pages

Narration: Ask your student for a narration from this reading. You may request that he say it aloud, write it down, or draw a narration.

Afternoon Occupation

Special Study: Instruct your child to observe one of his special study objects. Then, using the list you prepared, ask him some questions to foster an interest in looking at the thing more closely on his own. If your child needs help, offer to record his narration into his nature notebook for him.

Lesson 2: Natural History

Time: 20 minutes

Ask your student what he remembers from the last time he read *Rain, Hail, Sleet & Snow*.

You have been recording the humidity in the air by observing your pine cone's movement. Pine cones open and close depending on the moisture in the air, which helps seed dispersal. When the air is dry, the pine cone opens so the wind can catch its feather-light seeds and disperse them far from the parent tree. When the air is humid, the pine cone closes to prevent the seeds from becoming damp. A damp seed cannot travel far from the parent tree, so it has less opportunity to grow into a strong, healthy tree.

Student Read (or teacher if necessary): *Rain, Hail, Sleet & Snow*, chapter 8 "Dew and Frost."

Narration: Ask your student for a narration from this reading. You may request that he say it aloud, write it down, or draw a narration.

For Discussion: When the air is both humid and colder than 32-degrees, frost will form instead of dew. Have you ever looked at frost up close?

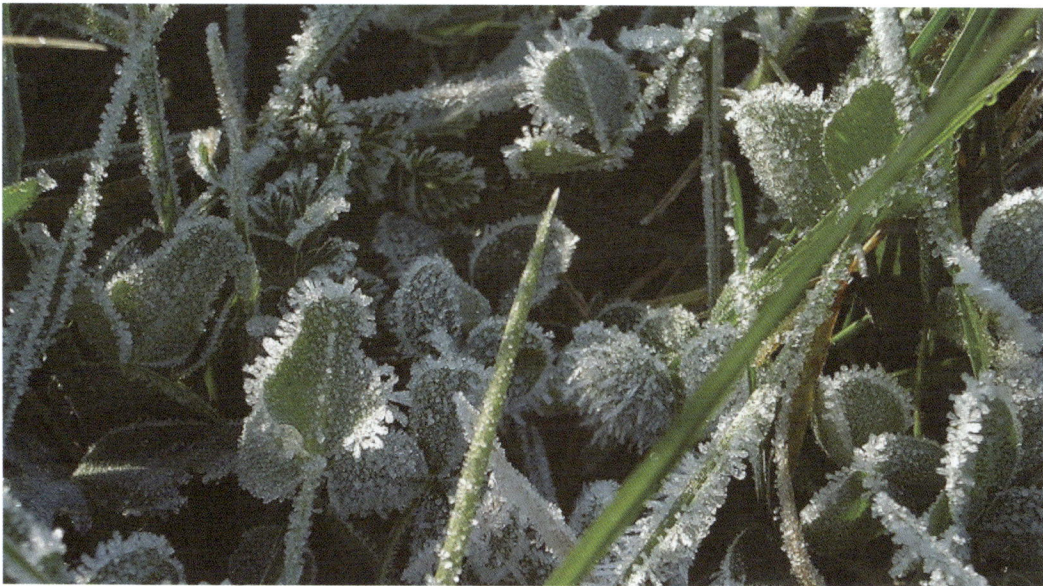

Source: Emmanuel Boutet - Own work, [CC BY-SA 3.0], via Wikimedia Commons

Afternoon Occupation

Special Study: Have your child take a few minutes to study the object he has chosen and then make notes and possibly a drawing in his nature notebook of something he has observed.

Lesson 3: Special Study Reading

Time: 30 minutes

Read: Special Study book; student read for about 10 minutes.

Narration: Ask your student for a narration from this reading. You may request it be oral, written, or drawn.

Afternoon Occupation

Nature Study: Have your child take a few minutes to observe his special study object or nature in general. Then make notes and possibly a drawing in his nature notebook of what he has observed. If you haven't completed an object lesson yet this week, do so today.

Painting: If your child has an interest, read John Muir Laws' article, "How to Paint Raindrops and Dew." (https://qrs.ly/37cmy9b)

TEACHER PREP

01
Prepare to do an object lesson on the next plant or animal of your child's chosen special study.

- Write out a few more questions from the lesson in *HoNS* on the special study topic your child is focusing on. Use these questions for reference when you go outside for a nature walk.

02
Gather the supplies needed for this week's activities.

- Ice cube
- Tongs or pliers
- Paper plate or construction paper
- Marker
- Scissors
- Stick pin
- Heat source, such as a light bulb or electric burner (use the latter only with parent permission and supervision)

03
Order books from the library.

- Do you need to renew your library books about your special study topic or get some new ones?

04
Schedule your weekly nature walk and outside time.

- Do not neglect this important time in your day because nature study is more than just the foundation for science. "*Consider, too, what an unequalled mental training the child-naturalist is getting for any study or calling under the sun–– the powers of attention, of discrimination, of patient pursuit, growing with his growth, what will they not fit him for?*" —Charlotte Mason, *Home Education*, p. 62

Lesson 1: Nature Lore

Time: 20 minutes

Read: Nature Lore book; 3-4 pages

Narration: Ask your student for a narration from this reading. You may request that he say it aloud, write it down, or draw a narration.

Afternoon Occupation

Special Study: Instruct your child to observe one of his special study objects. Then, using the list you prepared, ask him some questions to foster an interest in looking at the thing more closely on his own. If your child needs help, offer to record his narration into his nature notebook for him.

Lesson 2: Natural History

Time: 20 minutes

Ask your student what he remembers from the last time he read *Rain, Hail, Sleet & Snow.*

The Wind by Robert Louis Stevenson

I saw you toss the kites on high
And blow the birds about the sky;
And all around I heard you pass,
Like ladies' skirts across the grass--
> *O wind, a-blowing all day long,*
> *O wind, that sings so loud a song!*

I saw the different things you did,
But always you yourself you hid.
I felt you push, I heard you call,
I could not see yourself at all--
> *O wind, a-blowing all day long,*
> *O wind, that sings so loud a song!*

O you that are so strong and cold,
O blower, are you young or old?
Are you a beast of field and tree,
Or just a stronger child than me?
> *O wind, a-blowing all day long,*
> *O wind, that sings so loud a song!*

The wind is one of the main components of weather, but what causes the wind to blow in the first place?

Student Read (or teacher if necessary): "How the Sun Can Cause a Snowstorm" on the following page.

Narration: Ask your student for a narration from this reading. You may request that he say it aloud, write it down, or draw a narration.

Afternoon Occupation

Special Study: Have your child take a few minutes to study the object he has chosen and then make notes and possibly a drawing in his nature notebook of something he has observed.

How the Sun Can Cause a Snowstorm

On a warm summer day, it is easy to recognize that the sun is the cause of the weather in your area. But would you believe that the sun is also the cause of the snowstorms a region may receive? All the weather you experience, including wind, clouds, and precipitation, results from the atmosphere responding to the uneven heating of the earth by the sun.

Energy from the sun travels to the earth at 186,000 miles per second, taking only 8 minutes to reach its destination. Once there, some of its radiation is absorbed by the upper atmosphere, and some of it is reflected back to space. The remaining radiation passes through to heat the earth's surface.

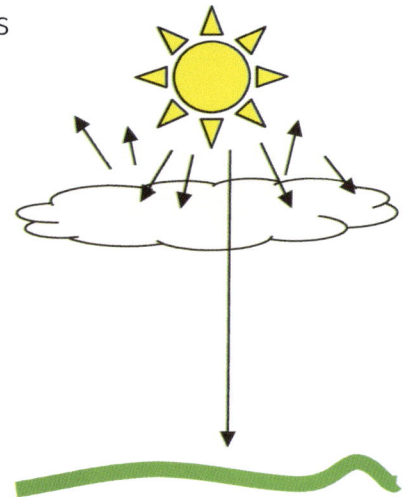

Not all surfaces absorb the sun's radiation to the same degree, however. Dark-colored objects absorb more radiation than light-colored objects. Because of this, you may prefer to wear a white shirt on a hot summer day. Also, rough and dry materials absorb more radiation than smooth and wet materials. Therefore, radiation absorbed by a dense forest or a desert, or an ocean of water, varies.

The slant of the sun's rays affects their intensity also. Consider the heat you feel from the sun at noon on a summer day, compared to the heat you feel when the sun is low in the sky in the evening on the same day. The same thing happens on a global scale. The sun is directly overhead at the equator, but its rays hit the northern and southern hemispheres at a slant. Therefore, Brazil receives more heat from the sun than Canada does. In addition, as our planet moves around the sun, the tilt of the earth's axis causes first the northern latitudes to lean toward the sun and then the southern latitudes to do so. The half that is tilted toward the sun experiences the warmer temperatures of summer. In comparison, the half that is tilted away from the sun experiences the cooler temperatures of winter.

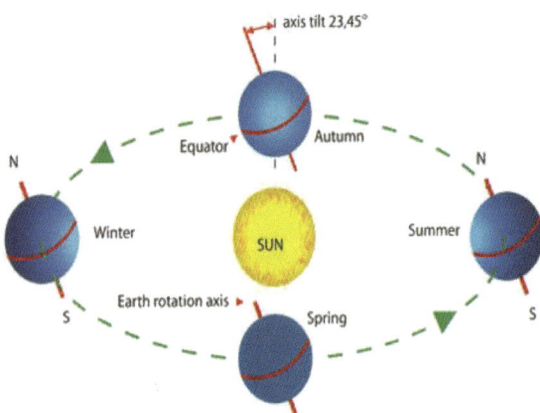

The uneven heating of the earth by the sun causes temperature differences from region to region. That, in turn, causes air currents (wind) to develop, which drives warm air to cooler areas. But the air that is moved from warmer areas to cooler regions can cause clouds and precipitation. Therefore, the snowstorm passing through your neighborhood today may have been caused by the sun's bright intensity over a location many miles away from you.

Lesson 3: Activity

Time: 30 minutes

In the last lesson, you learned that radiation from the sun warms the earth's surface and causes air currents to develop. Perform the following experiments to observe those currents.

Activity: Learn about air currents caused by the uneven heating of a surface.

Supplies Needed—

- Ice cube
- Tongs or pliers
- Paper plate or construction paper
- Marker
- Scissors
- Stick pin
- Heat source, such as a light bulb or electric burner (**use the latter only with parent permission and supervision**)

Procedure—

1. Hold the ice cube with the tongs or pliers.
2. Hold your hand just underneath the ice cube.
3. Slowly move your hand downward about a foot underneath the ice cube. Notice how far you can move your hand and still feel cool air.
4. Next, hold your hand just above the ice cube.
5. Slowly raise your hand about a foot above the ice cube. What do you feel now?
6. Notice how far you can move your hand above the ice cube and still feel cool air.
7. You may see mist around the ice cube. If so, notice which direction the mist is flowing from the ice cube.

You should have noticed that there was cooler air further from the underside of the ice cube than there was above it. This happened because the air that was cooled by the ice cube became dense and sank.

8. Starting from the center point of the paper plate, draw a spiral line until you reach the edge.
9. Cut along the line to create a paper snake.
10. You may need to cut a portion off if your snake hangs down much more than 2 feet. Otherwise, it may touch your heat source and create a fire.

11. Push a stick pin through the head of your snake. (The center of the plate.)
12. Turn on your heat source.
13. Hold your snake by the stick pin so it can turn freely, then dangle it over the heat source. (Please be sure not to touch the heat source with your snake as it may start a fire.)
14. Observe what happens.
15. Move your snake to the side of your heat source.
16. Observe what happens.

Hot air is lighter than cool air, therefore, it rises above it. As the air near your heat source rose up through your snake, it pushed on it and caused it to spin. When you moved your snake away from the heat source, it quit spinning as no air was pushing on it.

It is this movement of air, warm air rising and cool air moving in to take its place, that causes a current of air. On a much larger scale, it is the uneven temperatures on the surface of the earth that create massive convection currents to move air all around the planet.

Narration: Can you explain how the sun causes wind?

This activity was adapted fromThe Science Notebook: Heat - Part 2.

Afternoon Occupation

Nature Study: Have your child take a few minutes to observe his special study object or nature in general. Then make notes and possibly a drawing in his nature notebook of what he has observed. If you haven't completed an object lesson yet this week, do so today.

TEACHER PREP

01 Read a portion of the *Handbook of Nature Study* (*HoNS*).

- Write out a few more questions from the lesson on the special study topic your child is focusing on. Use these questions for reference when you go outside for a nature walk.
- If there are no more questions to write down from this lesson, see if there is another lesson that is related or considers the topic in a more general way. For instance, if your student has been studying Queen Anne's Lace (Lesson 148,) which is one of the specific weeds covered in *HoNS*, then you can look back at Lesson 135: Outline for the Study of a Weed.

02 Gather the supplies needed for this week's activities.

- None needed.

03 Schedule your weekly nature walk and outside time.

- Do you have a good rotation of places to walk? Are there some other places you would like to try out next term?
- Are you getting into the habit of establishing a goal for each nature walk?
- Did your kids make regular nature notebook entries this term? Do you need to figure out a better system so that it doesn't get forgotten?
- Are there any changes you would like to make next term?

Lesson 1: Nature Lore

Time: 20 minutes

Read: Nature Lore book; 3-4 pages

Narration: Ask your student for a narration from this reading. You may request that he say it aloud, write it down, or draw a narration.

Afternoon Occupation

Special Study: Instruct your child to observe one of his special study objects. Then, using the list you prepared, ask him some questions to foster an interest in looking at the thing more closely on his own. If your child needs help, offer to record his narration into his nature notebook for him.

Lesson 2: Natural History

Time: 20 minutes

Today you will complete your study of the weather by learning how the weather contributes to the water cycle.

Student Read (or teacher if necessary): *Rain, Hail, Sleet & Snow*, chapter 9 "Water Goes Up and Down."

Narration: Ask your student for a narration from this reading. You may request that he say it aloud, write it down, or draw a narration.

For Discussion: Study the diagram of the water cycle at the end of this chapter. Do you have any questions?

Optional Activities:

- Test the rate of evaporation in your home. Set two small Mason jars on the counter, with equal amounts of water in them. Cover one of them tightly with a lid. Watch them over the course of several days, comparing the water level of each.
- Watch the StudyJams video, "Water Cycle." (https://qrs.ly/kecmy9j, 3:27 min.)

Afternoon Occupation

Special Study: Have your child take a few minutes to study the object he has chosen and then make notes and possibly a drawing in his nature notebook of something he has observed.

Lesson 3: Special Study Reading

Time: 30 minutes

Read: Special Study book; student read for about 10 minutes.

Narration: Ask your student for a narration from this reading. You may request it be oral, written, or drawn.

Afternoon Occupation

Nature Study: Have your child take a few minutes to observe his special study object or nature in general. Then make notes and possibly a drawing in his nature notebook of what he has observed. If you haven't completed an object lesson yet this week, do so today.

Appendix

Observe the Weather

"Ring around the moon?
Rain real soon."

1. What is the weather like today? Is it sunny or cloudy? Is it warm or cool? Do you feel a light breeze or a strong wind? Does the air feel dry or moist? Can you see your breath?
2. Where is the sun in the sky? Where does it rise and set? Can you feel the sun's warmth? Compare the temperature of objects that are dark-colored, light-colored, rough, and smooth. Which is warmer? Which is cooler?
3. Are you sweating, or do you have goosebumps? How did you dress to go outside today?
4. What season is it? Are flowers blooming, or are leaves falling from the trees? What do you see, hear, smell, taste, and touch that you do not notice at other times of the year? What do you like to do this time of year?
5. Is the weather the same as it was yesterday? Is it the same as it was last month? If not, how is it different? Does the weather affect what you can do outside?

Clouds

"When clouds look like black smoke,
A wise man will put on his cloak."

1. Lie down outside and look for familiar shapes in the clouds. Do you see animals, people, or other forms? Describe what you see.
2. How tall are the clouds? Are they thick and puffy or thin and wispy? Are they light-colored or dark-colored? Are they moving? In which direction are they moving? Are all of the clouds moving in the same direction? Do you recognize what type of clouds you see? How much of the sky is covered by clouds?
3. View the sky's reflection through a pool of water, such as a pond, puddle, or a bowl of water. Can you see clouds in the water that you cannot see when you look at the sky directly?
4. Use binoculars to examine the clouds. (Do not look toward the sun as it will damage your eyes.) Do you see motion in the air around or within the cloud? Does it appear that the air is moving in different directions around different sets of clouds? How do the edges of the clouds look? Find some with soft edges and others with ragged edges.

Rain

"Thunder in the morning,
All day storming.
Thunder at night,
Traveler's delight."

1. Listen to the sound of raindrops on the roof or windows. What sound does the rain make?
2. How quickly is the rain falling? Is it sprinkling or falling heavily? Set an empty pan outside to collect the rain for an hour. How much water did you collect?
3. Are the raindrops big or small? Measure a raindrop by placing flour in a pan to a depth of 1-inch and then letting 15-20 raindrops fall into the pan. Use a sieve to remove the excess flour. The little lumps left behind are preserved raindrops. Carefully remove each one from the sieve and then measure them.
4. Do you see a puddle on a hard surface? Look at it again later in the day. Did some of the water from the puddle evaporate? You can draw a line around the edge of a puddle with chalk to see the change in size throughout the day.
5. Do you see a rainbow? What colors do you see? In what order do the colors appear? Is there a double rainbow? If so, in what order do the colors of the second rainbow appear? Make a rainbow by standing with your back to the sun and spraying a garden hose into the air.

Snow, Frost or Hail

"On a cold snowy day
Country folks say;
The old woman is picking her geese
Selling feathers a penny a piece."

1. Is the snow falling fast or slow? Does it seem heavy or light? Is it falling straight down, or is the wind blowing it sideways?
2. Is the snow wet or dry? Which would make a better snowman? How well does the snow stick together? How big of a snowball can you make?
3. Collect snowflakes on your mitten or a piece of black construction paper or felt and look at them with a magnifying glass. What sizes and shapes are the snowflakes?
4. How would you describe snow to someone who has never seen it?
5. Find out how much water is in the snow by filling a pan full of snow and then allowing it to melt by bringing it indoors or heating it on a stovetop.
6. Look at the frost on plants or car windows. Do you see any patterns? Look at it through a magnifying glass.
7. Dissect a hailstone by breaking it with a hammer and then observing it with a magnifying glass.

Wind

*"Wind before rain,
Fair weather again."*

1. Is the wind blowing? How can you tell the wind is blowing? Can you see it? Can you hear it?
2. How hard is the wind blowing? Is it moving the leaves or branches of the trees? Can you see smoke coming from a chimney? In what direction is the smoke moving? Do you have a flag pole? In what direction is the flag waving? From what direction is the wind blowing?
3. Do you feel the wind on your face? Is it ruffling your hair, or did it blow your hat away? What does it feel like when there is no wind at all?
4. Blow bubbles outside and then watch as the wind moves them.
5. On a windy day, spread petroleum jelly on a cookie sheet, then hold it up to the wind. Observe what you caught. Look closer by using a magnifying glass.

Seasons

*"The taller the weeds during the summer,
the deeper the snow in the winter."*

1. Are flowers blooming, or are leaves falling from the trees?
2. What do you see, hear, smell, taste, and touch that is only there this time of year?

About the Author

Nicole Williams learned about Charlotte Mason a few years after she began homeschooling and the same year she added three additional students to her schoolroom! It was a trial by fire that resulted in a refinement of Charlotte Mason's methods and philosophy in her home. More than a decade later, she has written a living science curriculum, teaches at conferences, and co-hosts the Charlotte Mason podcast A Delectable Education. Nicole enjoys working in her garden, collecting living books, hiking, reading, and listening to podcasts.

Other Titles in This Series

Form 2 (Grades 2-6)
Botany. The First Book of Plants by Alice Dickinson
Chemistry. Matter, Molecules, and Atoms by Bertha Morris Parker
Physics - Magnets. Magnets by Rocco V. Feravolo
Physics - Waves. The First Book of Sound by David Knight
Physics - Energy. The First Book of Electricity by Sam and Beryl Epstein
Engineering & Technology. The First Book of Machines by Walter Buehr
Astronomy. Find the Constellations by H.A. Rey
Weather. Rain, Hail, Sleet & Snow by Nancy Larrick
Geology. The First Book of the Earth by O. Irene Sevrey

Form 3-4 (Grades 7-9)
Biology. Men, Microscopes, and Living Things by Katherine B. Shippen
Botany. First Studies of Plant Life by George Francis Atkinson
Chemistry. The Mystery of the Periodic Table by Benjamin Wiker
Physics. Secrets of the Universe by Paul Fleisher
Engineering & Technology. Electronics for Kids by Øyvind Nydal Dahl
Astronomy. The Planets by Dava Sobel
Weather. Look at the Sky and Tell the Weather by Eric Sloane
Geology. Rocks, Rivers and the Changing Earth: A First Book About Geology by Herman and Nina Schneider

High School (Grades 9-12)
Biology, Anatomy part 1. The Body: A Guide for Occupants by Bill Bryson
Biology, Anatomy part 2. The Body: A Guide for Occupants by Bill Bryson
Biology, Ecology.
Biology, Origins.
Chemistry, part 1. Wonders of Chemistry by A. Frederick Collins
Chemistry, part 2. Wonders of Chemistry by A. Frederick Collins
Chemistry, part 3. Wonders of Chemistry by A. Frederick Collins
Physics, part 1. For the Love of Physics by Walter Lewin
Physics, part 2. For the Love of Physics by Walter Lewin
Physics, part 3/Astrophysics. For the Love of Physics by Walter Lewin
Geology. Aerial Geography by Mary Caperton Morton
Weather.

Printed in Great Britain
by Amazon

78793785R00040